The ASSASSINATION of ABRAHAM LINCOLN

A DAY THAT CHANGED AMERICA

by Jessica Gunderson

CAPSTONE PRESS
a capstone imprint

Capstone Captivate is published by Capstone Press, an imprint of Capstone.
1710 Roe Crest Drive, North Mankato, Minnesota 56003
www.capstonepub.com

Library of Congress Cataloging-in-Publication Data
Names: Gunderson, Jessica, author.
Title: The assassination of Abraham Lincoln : a day that changed America / by Jessica Gunderson.
Description: North Mankato, Minnesota : Capstone Press, [2022] | Series: Days that changed America | Includes bibliographical references and index. | Audience: Ages 8-11 | Audience: Grades 4-6 | Summary: "On April 14, 1865, only days after the Civil War had come to a close, a gunshot rang out in Ford's Theatre and President Abraham Lincoln slumped forward in his seat. Hours later, the United States had lost its leader. Now readers can step back in time to learn about what led up to the assassination plot, how the fateful evening unfolded, and the ways in which one tragic day changed America forever"-- Provided by publisher.
Identifiers: LCCN 2021026076 (print) | LCCN 2021026077 (ebook) |
  ISBN 9781663905796 (hardcover) | ISBN 9781663920775 (paperback) |
  ISBN 9781663905765 (pdf) | ISBN 9781663905789 (kindle edition)
Subjects: LCSH: Lincoln, Abraham, 1809-1865--Assassination--Juvenile literature.
Classification: LCC E457.5 .G858 2022 (print) | LCC E457.5 (ebook) | DDC 973.7092--dc23
LC record available at https://lccn.loc.gov/2021026076
LC ebook record available at https://lccn.loc.gov/2021026077

Image Credits
Associated Press: North Wind Picture Archives, 12; Getty Images: Ed Vebell, 16, Grafissimo, 6, ilbusca, 9; Library of Congress: cover, 11, 18, 24, Alexander Gardner, 10, 22, Brady's National Photographic Portrait Galleries, 13, Rare Book and Special Collections Division/The Alfred Whital Stern Collection of Lincolniana, 5, 15, 17, 20, Ridgway Glover, 19; Newscom: Everett Collection, 21; Shutterstock: Atoly (design element), cover and throughout, David Brickner, 27, Everett Collection, 8, 25, Marzolino, 26; Smithsonian Institution: National Portrait Gallery, 7, 14, 23

Editorial Credits
Editor: Kristy Stark; Media Researcher: Svetlana Zhurkin; Production Specialist: Kathy McColley

Consultant Credits
Dr. W. Marvin Dulaney, Associate Professor of History Emeritus, University of Texas, Arlington

All internet sites appearing in back matter were available and accurate when this book was sent to press.

TABLE OF CONTENTS

Words in **bold** are in the glossary.

On April 14, 1865, Ford's Theatre was packed. Onstage, actors performed the play *Our American Cousin*. After four long years of war, the people of Washington, D.C., were ready to laugh.

Then, a very special guest arrived. It was Abraham Lincoln, president of the United States. The crowd stood and clapped. The president and the first lady took their balcony seats in the theater's presidential box.

The audience roared with laughter at a funny line in the play. A gunshot rang out! The president slumped in his seat. A man yelled. He leaped from the balcony and ran out the back door.

The stunned audience realized what had happened. The president had been shot! Some chased after the assassin. But he was long gone. Others rushed to help the president. Lincoln was lying on the balcony floor, bleeding. The next day, he would die and leave a nation changed forever.

After shooting Lincoln, Booth jumped over the railing of the balcony and landed on the main stage.

CHAPTER 1

A DIVIDED NATION

In 1860, Abraham Lincoln was elected president of the United States. At the time, the practice of enslaving others was legal in southern states.

Many enslaved people were forced to pick cotton.

The Black people who became enslaved were kidnapped from Africa. Then, they were taken across the Atlantic Ocean and sold to people. They were forced to work on large farms, in homes, and at seaports. The conditions were awful. Enslaved people received no pay. They were treated as property, not as human beings.

Abraham Lincoln was a politician from Illinois. He did not like slavery. Southern enslavers worried that he would **abolish** slavery if he became president. After Lincoln won the election, 11 southern states **seceded** from the **Union**. These states formed the Confederate States of America.

A photograph of Abraham Lincoln, taken in February 1860, helped convince people that he would be a good candidate for president.

In April 1861, war broke out between the **Confederacy** and the Union. At first, Lincoln wanted only to reunite the two sides. But then he realized more people would support the Union if it were fighting against slavery. In 1863, President Lincoln gave the Emancipation Proclamation. It declared that all enslaved people in the Confederate states were free. Slavery was still legal in border states that did not join the Confederacy. The Proclamation was important, but it would not free any enslaved people until after the war. The Proclamation also allowed Black people to serve in the Union Army. Nearly 200,000 Black soldiers ended up serving.

A Black family arrived at a Union army camp in 1863.

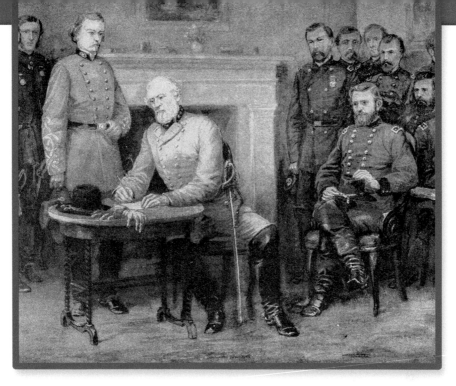

On April 9, 1865, General Lee surrendered to General Grant in the Appomattox Courthouse in Virginia.

In 1864, Lincoln was elected again. On April 9, 1865, the Civil War ended with Confederate surrender. About 700,000 people were dead. Thousands more were wounded. More than 4 million enslaved people became free. The nation had been torn apart by the war. President Lincoln aimed to put the country back together.

CHAPTER 2

THE PLAN

John Wilkes Booth was an actor in Washington, D.C. He lived in the North, but he supported the Confederacy. He did not believe enslaved people should be free. He also did not believe Black people should have equal rights. He hated Abraham Lincoln for his efforts in freeing enslaved people.

John Wilkes Booth in 1865

FORD'S THEATRE

TENTH STREET, ABOVE E.

SEASON II .... WEEK XXXI .... NIGHT 191
WHOLE NUMBER OF NIGHTS, 495.

JOHN T. FORD .... PROPRIETOR AND MANAGER
(Also of Holliday St. Theatre, Baltimore, and Academy of Music, Phil'a.)
Stage Manager .... J. B. WRIGHT
Treasurer .... H. CLAY FORD

Friday Evening, April 14th, 1865

THIS EVENING,

The Performance will be honored by the presence of

PRESIDENT LINCOLN

BENEFIT!

—AND—

LAST NIGHT

OF MISS

LAURA KEENE

THE DISTINGUISHED MANAGERESS, AUTHORESS AND ACTRESS,
Supported by

MR. JOHN DYOTT

AND

MR. HARRY HAWK

TOM TAYLOR'S CELEBRATED ECCENTRIC COMEDY

As originally produced in America by Miss Keene, and performed by her upwards of

ONE THOUSAND NIGHTS,

ENTITLED

OUR AMERICAN

COUSIN

FLORENCE TRENCHARD	MISS LAURA KEENE	
(Her Original Character.)		
Abel Murcott, Clerk to Attorney	John Dyott	
Asa Trenchard	Harry Hawk	
Sir Edward Trenchard	T. C. GOURLAY	
Lord Dundreary	E. A. EMERSON	
Mr. Coyle, Attorney	J. MATTHEWS	
Lieutenant Vernon, R. N	W. J. FERGUSON	
Captain De Boots	C. BYRNES	
Binney	G. G. SPEAR	
Buddicomb, a Valet	J. H. EVANS	
John Whicker, a gardener	J. L. DeBONAY	
Rasper, a groom		
Bailiffs	G. A. PARKHURST and L. JOHNSON	
Mary Trenchard	Miss J. GOURLAY	
Mrs. Mountchessington	Mrs. H. MUZZY	
Augusta	Miss H. TRUEMAN	
Georgina	Miss M. HART	
Sharpe	Mrs. J. H. EVANS	
Skillet	Miss M. GOURLAY	

SATURDAY EVENING, APRIL 15,

BENEFIT of Miss JENNIE GOURLAY

When will be presented BOURCICAULT'S Great Sensational Drama,

THE OCTOROON

Easter Monday, April 17, Engagement of the YOUNG AMERICAN TRAGEDIAN,

EDWIN ADAMS

FOR TWELVE NIGHTS ONLY.

THE PRICES OF ADMISSION:
Orchestra $1.00
Dress Circle and Parquette 75
Family Circle 25
Private Boxes .... $6 and $10

J. R. FORD, Business Manager.

H. Polkinhorn & Son, Printers, D street, near 7th, Washington, D. C.

Booth wanted revenge. On the morning of April 14, he learned that President Lincoln would be at Ford's Theatre that night. He saw his chance.

Booth had performed many plays at Ford's Theatre. He knew the staff, so he could enter without suspicion. He also knew the layout of the theater and could escape easily out the back door.

An ad for the April 14, 1865, performance of *Our American Cousin* mentioned that Lincoln would be attending.

Ford's Theatre opened in 1862.

Before the play began, Booth went to the theater. He placed a piece of wood inside the presidential box. He would use it to wedge the door shut behind him so no one could come in. He tied up a horse behind the theater. He hoped to gallop away before anyone could catch him. Then, he went to the tavern next-door to wait.

A LARGER PLOT

John Wilkes Booth wanted other U.S. leaders dead too. When he found out about Lincoln attending the play, he gathered some **accomplices** together. They planned to kill three other men that night, April 14. The men were General Ulysses S. Grant, Vice President Andrew Johnson, and Secretary of State William Seward. The plan did not work out. Grant was supposed to attend the play with Lincoln. But he didn't. The man assigned to kill Johnson changed his mind. Seward was attacked at his home but survived.

General Ulysses S. Grant

CHAPTER 3

THE DEATH OF LINCOLN

The brisk April breeze rushed into Ford's Theatre as the front entrance swung open. President Abraham Lincoln strode through the door. He was with his wife, Mary, and a young couple, Henry Rathbone and Clara Harris. They made their way into the crowded theater. The play had already begun.

Abraham and Mary Todd Lincoln on a walk around the White House

Booth sneaked into the presidential box and waited for the perfect time to fire the pistol.

The crowd hushed when they saw the president. The orchestra began to play "Hail to the Chief." The president took his seat, and the play continued.

Over an hour later, the door to the theater opened once more. John Wilkes Booth entered. He carried a pistol and a knife in his pocket. Booth nodded at the clerk and continued into the theater. Then, he made his way to the presidential box. He quietly slipped inside.

Booth knew the play by heart. He waited for a funny line. The audience broke into laughter. Booth stepped up to Lincoln. He aimed his pistol at the back of Lincoln's head and fired.

The president slumped in his seat. Mary Lincoln screamed. Henry Rathbone lunged at Booth. But Booth had his knife ready. He stabbed Rathbone. Then, he leaped over the railing of the balcony. When he hit the floor, his leg broke beneath him. But he ignored the pain and ran out the back door.

The audience was alarmed and confused. Some recognized the actor Booth and thought the uproar was part of the play. Others realized Lincoln had been shot.

People reported that Booth's foot got stuck in an American flag as he jumped over the balcony railing.

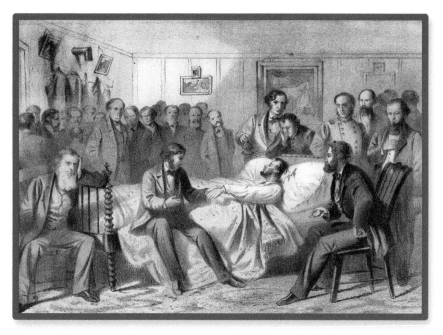

Government officials arrived at Lincoln's bedside.

FACT

Abraham Lincoln was the first president to be assassinated. Three other U.S. presidents have been assassinated—James Garfield (1881), William McKinley (1901), and John F. Kennedy (1963).

Lincoln hadn't woken up, but he was still alive. A group of men carried him out of the theater to a house across the street. They placed him on a small bed. Several doctors tended to him throughout the night. But Lincoln never woke up. He died at 7:22 the next morning on April 15, 1865.

CHAPTER 4

THE NATION REACTS

News of Lincoln's death was **telegraphed** around the country. Newspapers announced his death on the front page. The nation was shocked. **Mourners** throughout the country hung wreaths on their doors. The nation stopped celebrating the end of the war.

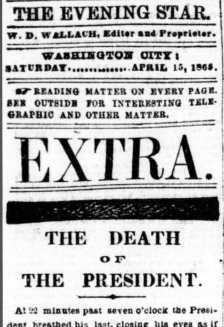

An article from *The Evening Star* announcing Lincoln's death

THE EVENING STAR.

W. D. WALLACH, Editor and Proprietor.

WASHINGTON CITY:
SATURDAY...........APRIL 15, 1865.

☞ READING MATTER ON EVERY PAGE. SEE OUTSIDE FOR INTERESTING TELE-GRAPHIC AND OTHER MATTER.

EXTRA.

THE DEATH
OF
THE PRESIDENT.

At 22 minutes past seven o'clock the President breathed his last, closing his eyes as if falling to sleep, and his countenance assuming an expression of perfect serenity. There were no indications of pain, and it was not known that he was dead until the gradually decreasing respiration ceased altogether.

Rev. Dr. Gurley, (of the New York Avenue Presbyterian Church,) immediately on its being ascertained that life was extinct, knelt at the bedside and offered an impressive prayer, which was responded to by all present.

Dr. Gurley then proceeded to the front parlor, where Mrs. Lincoln, Capt. Robert Lincoln, Mr. John Hay, the Private Secretary, and others, were waiting, where he again offered prayer for the consolation of the family.

The death of the president had mixed reactions. Many Americans were heartbroken. Some northerners disliked Lincoln. And many southerners had viewed him as an enemy throughout the war. Some celebrated. Other southerners were uncertain. They knew Lincoln's goal had been to reunite the country. But now they worried the new leadership might punish the South more severely.

Lincoln's death hit Black Americans hard. Lincoln was a symbol of their freedom. Now that he was dead, they worried they might be enslaved again. For the entire country, the future was uncertain.

The Illinois State House was covered with black and white mourning cloth for Lincoln's funeral.

On April 19, a funeral service was held in the White House. Then, Lincoln's body traveled by train over 1,600 miles (2,575 kilometers) to his hometown of Springfield, Illinois. The train made several stops along the way so mourners could pay respects. Millions of Americans viewed Lincoln's casket.

Thousands of mourners lined up to watch the funeral procession.

Meanwhile, a large manhunt was going on for the assassin. Booth escaped capture for 12 days. He hid in the Maryland wilderness as he made his way to Virginia. Sometimes, people helped him. Finally, authorities found him. He was hiding in a barn in Virginia. The barn was set on fire. Booth was shot. He soon died.

FACT
....
A $100,000 reward (equal to more than $1.5 million today) was offered for Booth's capture.

Soldiers dragged Booth from the burning barn after he was shot.

CHAPTER 5

THE AFTERMATH

Throughout the war, Lincoln often thought about ways to reunite the country after Union victory. In 1863, he laid out a plan. Southern states could rejoin the Union once 10 percent of their voters pledged allegiance to the United States. He also wanted southern state governments to protect the freedom of the former enslaved. After the war was over, he spoke about voting rights for Black Union soldiers.

Lincoln's last official portrait, taken in February 1865

Andrew Johnson was sworn in as president a few hours after Lincoln's death.

But Lincoln did not have a chance to put his plans into action. After Lincoln's death, Vice President Andrew Johnson took on the role of president. He was now in charge of bringing the southern states back into the Union. This was called Reconstruction.

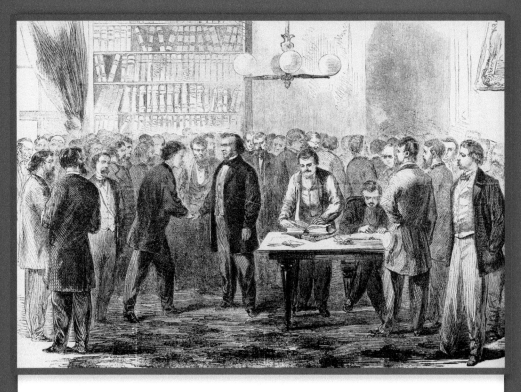

President Andrew Johnson eventually pardoned more than 13,500 rebels.

> **FACT**
> ....
> Many southern states had laws that said Black Americans could not be taught to read or write.

President Johnson had different ideas than Lincoln. He didn't believe in equal rights for Black Americans. He **pardoned** many Confederate leaders. He was also against government **oversight** of southern states. Instead, he allowed southern states to set up their own governments. This resulted in many former Confederate leaders taking office.

Southern state governments passed many state laws that discriminated against Black people. These laws were called black codes. Black codes kept Black southerners from voting and owning land or guns. Some black codes required Black Americans to have written proof of a job or they could be fined money or arrested.

In 1877, Reconstruction officially ended. The failed Reconstruction attempt led to more unfair laws. Jim Crow laws separated white people and Black people in schools, restaurants, and other public places.

A former enslaved man was auctioned to pay a legal fine after being arrested in 1867.

One hundred years after Lincoln's death, the Civil Rights Movement of the 1960s began. The movement helped get rid of many laws that discriminated against Black citizens. But people of color still face discrimination and poverty today, and the fight for equality continues.

JOHNSON AND RECONSTRUCTION

Andrew Johnson was a southerner. He was chosen as Lincoln's running mate to show unity between the North and South. As president, Johnson argued with cabinet members and Congress on Reconstruction issues. He **vetoed** bills aimed at protecting Black people. Then he illegally fired Secretary of War Edwin Stanton. Congress voted on removing Johnson from office. He was one vote away from being removed.

In 1868, Johnson became the first president to almost be removed from office.

In 2020, protesters gathered in an effort to raise awareness for social justice issues, continuing the fight for equality.

Abraham Lincoln was assassinated at a crucial point in the nation's history. His death changed the way the U.S. would move forward from its broken past.

TIMELINE

1565: Enslaved people are brought to North America for the first time.

1808: The United States bans enslaved persons from being brought in from other countries to be sold.

FEBRUARY 12, 1809: Abraham Lincoln is born in Kentucky.

SEPTEMBER 1850: The Compromise of 1850 is reached. It was a major compromise over slavery, which included admitting California as a free state and the abolition of the slave trade in Washington, D.C.

NOVEMBER 6, 1860: Abraham Lincoln is elected the sixteenth president of the United States.

DECEMBER 20, 1860: South Carolina secedes from the United States. Ten more states will follow.

APRIL 12, 1861: The Civil War begins when shots are fired on U.S. troops in Charleston, South Carolina.

JANUARY 1, 1863: President Lincoln issues the Emancipation Proclamation, declaring all enslaved in the seceded states are free.

1864: John Wilkes Booth begins plotting to kidnap Abraham Lincoln. Later, he considers assassinating the president.

APRIL 9, 1865: The Civil War ends when Confederate General Robert E. Lee surrenders to U.S. General Ulysses S. Grant.

APRIL 14, 1865: Booth shoots Lincoln at Ford's Theatre in Washington, D.C. Lincoln dies the next day.

APRIL 26, 1865: Booth is shot and killed in Virginia after a widespread manhunt.

1870: All former Confederate states are readmitted into the Union.

1877: Reconstruction officially ends. Over the next century, laws discriminating against Black Americans are passed in many areas of the former Confederacy.

1964-1965: The Civil Rights Act and the Voting Rights Act finally give legal equality to Black Americans.

GLOSSARY

abolish (uh-BOL-ish)—to do away with completely

accomplice (uh-KOM-pliss)—someone who works with another in wrongdoing

Confederacy (kuhn-FE-druh-see)—the Confederate States of America, made up of 11 southern states that left the United States to form their own government

mourner (MORN-er)—a person who is grieving, especially over someone's death

oversight (oh-vur-SITE)—the act of directing work that is being done

pardon (PAHR-duhn)—an act of official forgiveness for a serious offense

secede (si-SEED)—to formally withdraw from a group or an organization, often to form another organization

telegraph (TEL-uh-graf)—to send through an electronic system for sending messages over wires

Union (YOON-yuhn)—the United States of America; also the northern states that fought against the southern states in the Civil War

veto (VEE-toh)—to refuse to approve, which prevents a measure from taking effect

READ MORE

Dunlavey, Ryan, and Fred Van Lente. *Action Presidents: Abraham Lincoln!* New York: HarperCollins, 2018.

Ghafoerkhan, Olivia. *Reconstruction.* Lake Elmo, MN: Focus Readers, 2020.

Shulman, Mark. *Abraham Lincoln: Defender of the Union!* San Diego: Portable Press, 2019.

INTERNET SITES

Abraham Lincoln Historical Society
abraham-lincoln-history.org/

Ford's Theatre: Lincoln's Assassination
fords.org/lincolns-assassination/

Lincoln Home National Historic Site
nps.gov/liho/index.htm

INDEX